P9-DUE-151

SIMPLY SCIENCE

Hot and Cold

by Darlene R. Stille

Content Advisers: Terrence E. Young Jr., M.Ed., M.L.S.,
Jefferson Parish (La.) Public Schools, and Janann Jenner, Ph.D.

Reading Adviser: Dr. Linda D. Labbo,
Department of Reading Education, College of Education,
The University of Georgia

COMPASS POINT BOOKS

Minneapolis, Minnesota

Compass Point Books
3722 West 50th Street, #115
Minneapolis, MN 55410

Visit Compass Point Books on the Internet at *www.compasspointbooks.com* or e-mail your
request to *custserv@compasspointbooks.com*

Photographs ©:

International Stock/Wayne Aldridge, cover; International Stock/Bob Firth, cover; Rob and Ann Simpson, 4, 28; Photo Network/
Eric R. Berndt, 5; Unicorn Stock Photos/Aneal Vohra, 7; Unicorn Stock Photos/Ted Rose, 8; Tom Pantages, 9; Unicorn Stock
Photos/Dede Gilman, 10; Ed Robinson/Tom Stack and Associates, 11; David Falconer, 12; Unicorn Stock Photos/Tom McCarthy,
15; Photo Network/Henryk T. Kaiser, 16; Terry Donnelly/Tom Stack and Associates, 17; Eric Anderson/Visuals Unlimited, 18, 19,
20; Unicorn Stock Photos/Judy Hile, 21; Greg Vaughn/Tom Stack and Associates, 22; Science VU/API/Visuals Unlimited, 23;
Mark Allen Stack/Tom Stack and Associates, 24; Bill Beatty/Visuals Unlimited, 25; Unicorn Stock Photos/Mark Romesser, 26;
Unicorn Stock Photos/Martin R. Jones, 27; Unicorn Stock Photos/Marie Mills/D. Cummings, 29.

Editors: E. Russell Primm, Emily J. Dolbear, and Melissa Stewart
Photo Researcher: Svetlana Zhurkina
Photo Selector: Matthew Eisentrager-Warner
Designer: Bradfordesign, Inc.

Library of Congress Cataloging-in-Publication Data

Stille, Darlene R.
    Hot and cold / by Darlene Stille.
      p. cm. — (Simply science)
    Includes bibliographical references and index.
    ISBN 0-7565-0090-7 (hardcover : lib. bdg.)
      1. Heat—Juvenile literature. 2. Cold—Juvenile literature. [1. Temperature—Experiments. 2. Heat—
Experiments. 3. Cold—Experiments. 4. Experiments.] I. Title. II. Simply science (Minneapolis, Minn.)
    QC256 .S75 2001
    536—dc21   00-010941

© 2001 by Compass Point Books
All rights reserved. No part of this book may be reproduced without written permission from the publisher. The publisher takes no
responsibility for the use of any of the materials or methods described in this book, nor for the products thereof.
Printed in the United States of America.

Table of Contents

Feeling Hot or Cold

We all know how hot or cold feels. A bowl of soup feels hot. The wind on a winter day feels cold. Fire is hot. Ice is cold. But do you know why things feel hot or cold? Things feel hot because they have lots of heat. Things feel cold because they give up heat energy.

People feel hot during warm summer days.

A child feels the coldness of snow.

Thermometers

Is it so cold outdoors that you need a coat? To find out, you can look at a thermometer. A thermometer can tell you the temperature of the air outside.

How hot is it inside your house? Do you need to turn on the air conditioner? A thermometer can also tell you this.

The numbers on a thermometer tell you how much heat is in the air. Some thermometers give the temperature in a scale, or system, called Fahrenheit.

Other thermometers use the Celsius system. Many thermometers

Outdoor thermometers tell us how warm or cold it is outside.

have both Fahrenheit and Celsius
scales.

Most thermometers are made of
a glass tube with **liquid** inside. The
liquid in the tube goes up when the
air gets warmer. The liquid in the tube
goes down when the air gets colder.

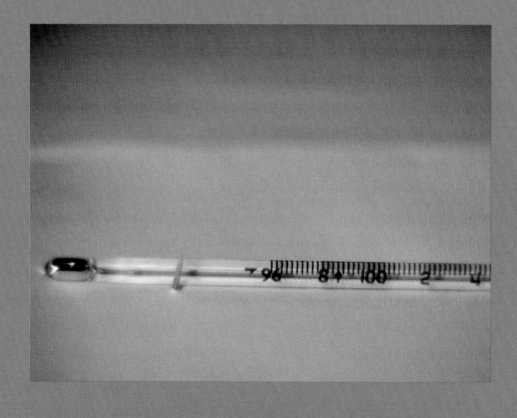

Some other kinds of thermometers
are round. They look a bit like clocks.
A hand points to the temperature.

This thermometer has a hand.

This thermometer has liquid inside and measures body temperature.

Other thermometers have a tiny window with the numbers displayed. The number inside the window tells you the temperature. This kind of thermometer is the safest kind for taking body temperature.

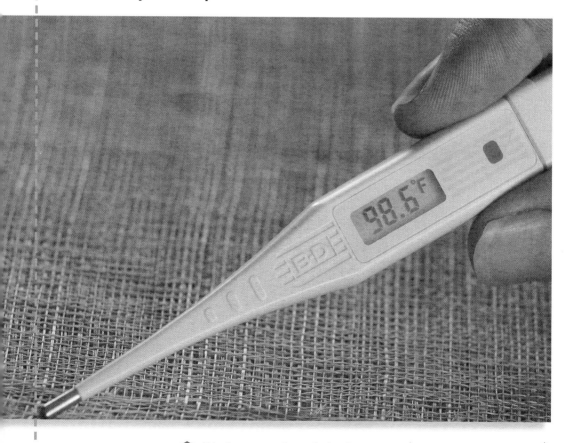

▲ This thermometer has a display that tells the temperature of the body.

We wear bathing suits ▶ during the summer heat.

Taking the Temperature

If the temperature is 100 degrees Fahrenheit (100°F), it is very hot outdoors. You should wear shorts or a bathing suit. When it is 100°F, it is 38 degrees Celsius (38°C).

If the temperature is 32°F, it is very cold outdoors. You should wear a heavy coat, a hat, and mittens. When it is 32°F, it is 0°C.

Some thermometers can tell you the temperature indoors and outdoors. Most people like the temperature indoors to be around 70°F. When it is 70°F, it is 21°C. This is called room temperature. At room temperature, most people like to wear long pants and a light shirt.

There are many uses for thermometers in your house. You can use a thermometer to check the temperature of food cooking in the oven. You can also

◀ *In many parts of the world, a heavy coat is necessary during the winter.*

use a thermometer to be sure your refrigerator is cold enough.

Thermometers are also used to take the temperature of your body. When you are healthy, your body temperature is about 98.6°F, or 37°C. That's pretty warm! If you have a temperature of more than 1°F (0.5°C) above normal, you might have a fever.

A thermometer tells us when we have a fever. ▷

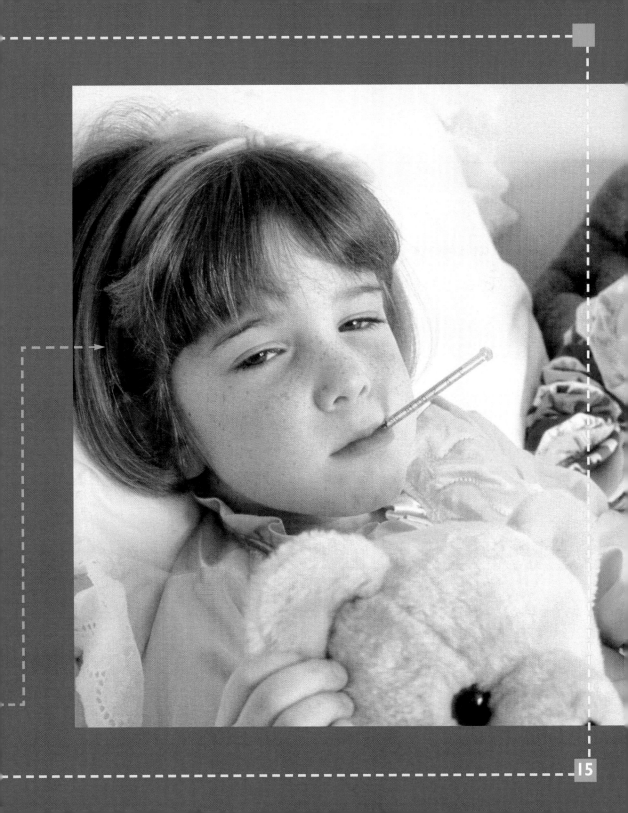

How Temperature Changes Things

Some things are in a liquid form at room temperature. Water is a good example. The water you drink is a liquid. If you cool water down, it turns into ice. Ice is a **solid**. If you heat water, it turns into steam. Steam is a **gas**.

◀ *Water is a liquid.*

Steam escapes from a geyser in snowy Yellowstone National Park. ▶

Would you like to see water change right in front of your eyes? Take some ice cubes from the freezer and put them into a pan. Ask an adult to help you warm the pan on the stove. Now watch what happens.

Ice is frozen water.

Ice melts in a pan as the stove heats it up.

When the pan gets hot, the ice cubes start to melt. The ice cubes turn into liquid water. When the water in the pan gets very hot, it starts to bubble. The water turns into steam and rises into the air.

All the water will turn into steam if you leave the pan boiling on the hot stove. What started as solid ice cubes will quickly turn into a gas that just floats away.

Freezing and Melting

When water cools to 32°F (0°C), it turns into solid ice. That temperature is the **freezing point** of water.

When ice is warmed to 32°F (0°C), it turns into liquid water. That temperature is the **melting point** of ice. Melting and freezing points are the same.

Steam is water in gas form.

Water freezes at 32°F (0°C).

Anything can melt or freeze. But different things have different melting and freezing points. Even rocks can melt and become liquid. But the temperature must be very, very hot.

Rocks melt into lava at very high temperatures.

Boiling and Burning

Water turns into steam at 212°F (100°C). That temperature is the **boiling point** of water. Other things have other boiling points. Some boiling points are low. Some boiling points are high. Iron has a boiling point of 4,982°F (2,750°C)!

Great heat is required to melt some things such as steel.

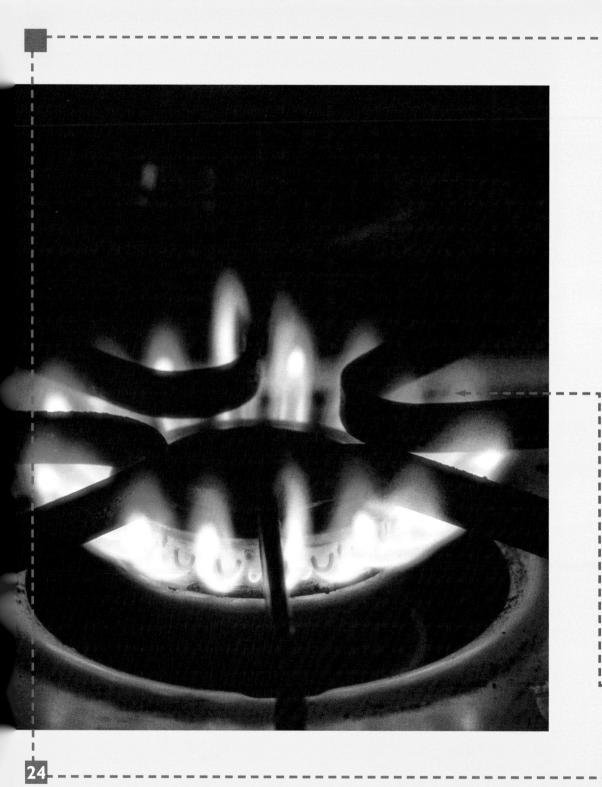

Some things burn when they get very hot. The temperature needed to make something burn is called the **ignition point**. Paper and wood are solid things that will burn. Some gases, such as natural gas, will burn. Some liquids will burn too. Kerosene is a liquid that burns. It is used in lamps and lanterns.

We use natural gas in our stoves to heat food.

Burning wood gives off heat. ▶

Heating and Cooling

The sun gives off heat. The heat rays travel through space to warm Earth.

Fire gives off heat. Have you ever watched a grown-up cook hot dogs over a campfire? Heat travels from the fire to the hot dogs.

An electric heater warms the air in a room. The warm air moves away from the heater into the room.

The sun's rays reach Earth.

Small heaters are often used to warm rooms.

Then more cold air passes through the heater, warms up, and moves away. Soon the whole room is warm.

Heat always moves from warmer things to cooler things. That's why your dinner gets cold if you don't eat it. The air around your meat and vegetables is cooler than the food. So, the heat moves out into the room, and your food cools down.

A refrigerator or freezer takes heat out of food. Air conditioners take heat out of air.

Hurry and eat or dinner will get cold!

Hot, Cold, and You

Heat from a furnace makes your house warm in the winter. Heat from a stove lets you cook food. You use hot water to take a bath and wash your clothes. A cold refrigerator keeps your food fresh for many days. Cold air from air conditioners helps you sleep on hot summer nights. Stop and think of all the ways you use hot and cold every day.

A hot bath can be relaxing . . . and fun!

Glossary

boiling point—the temperature at which something changes from a liquid to a gas

freezing point—the temperature at which something changes from a liquid to a solid

gas—a material that can flow and takes on the shape of the container it is in. Most gases can't be seen.

ignition point—the temperature at which an object starts to burn

liquid—a material that feels wet, can flow, and takes on the shape of the container it is in

melting point—the temperature at which an object changes from a solid to a liquid

solid—a material that has its own shape and is usually hard

Did You Know?

- Before electric refrigerators, people kept food cool in an icebox and had giant blocks of ice delivered every week.

- We could not live without heat from the sun, but the sun can also give us a painful burn. That's why it is important to use sunscreen.

- Fahrenheit, a scale for measuring temperatures, was developed by a German scientist named Gabriel D. Fahrenheit.

Want to Know More?

At the Library

Challoner, Jack. *Hot and Cold*. Austin, Tex.: Raintree Steck-Vaughn, 1996.

Hewitt, Sally. *Solid, Liquid, or Gas*. Danbury, Conn.: Children's Press, 2000.

Wick, Walter. *A Drop of Water*. New York: Scholastic, 1997.

On the Web

Make a Thermometer

http://www.energy.ca.gov/education/projects/projects-html/thermometer.html

For information about how to make and use your own thermometer

The Weather Channel

http://www.weather.com/homepage.html

For the temperature of cities in the United States and other countries

Through the Mail

Farmers' Almanac Order Desk

P.O. Box 1609

Mount Hope Avenue

Lewiston, ME 04241

To order a copy of this seasonal guide

On the Road

Museum of Science

Science Park

Boston, MA 02114-1099

617/723-2500

To check out exhibits that explore many different areas of science

Index

About the Author

Darlene R. Stille is a science editor and writer. She has lived in Chicago, Illinois, all her life. When she was in high school, she fell in love with science. While attending the University of Illinois, she discovered that she also enjoyed writing. Today she feels fortunate to have a career that allows her to pursue both her interests. Darlene R. Stille has written more than thirty books for young people.